Peter the Puffin

By

Anthony Mitchell

New Generation **Publishing**

Chapter One: A New Puffling

Mother Puffin had been sitting for what seemed like ages on her egg. Gradually, however, she began to realise that something strange was happening. She lifted herself off the egg and looked at it curiously. There was a tapping noise coming from inside, as if something was trying to get out. She became very excited.

She was inside a small chamber at the end of her burrow. There was very little space. When puffins get excited they flap their wings. This was not a good idea inside a burrow. Showers of dirt quickly filled the chamber. Mother Puffin had dirt in her eyes, dirt up her nose and dirt in her mouth. In fact she was covered in dirt.

At this moment, Father Puffin came waddling down the tunnel leading to the chamber. He'd been fishing and had caught several sand eels. He had them firmly in his bill because some were still squirming. He put the sand eels on the floor of the burrow and looked at Mother Puffin.

"What have you been doing?" he asked her, peering through the clouds of dust.

"Oh, I'm so excited," Mother Puffin replied trying not to choke, "I think our puffling (baby puffins are called pufflings) is about to hatch."

She continued flapping her wings. Poor Father Puffin was soon covered in dirt as well.

"Calm down!" he spluttered. "You're making a sandstorm, I can hardly breathe."

Mother Puffin stopped flapping her wings. The egg was by now covered with a thin layer of sand.

"Oh dear!" she exclaimed. "What a silly puffin I am!"

Mother Puffin then started brushing the sand off the egg with one of her wings. With sand in his eyes Father Puffin blinked hard and coughed a few times. He then decided to have a look for himself. There was just enough room for him to squeeze past Mother Puffin.

Father Puffin looked at the egg carefully and then cocked his ear to see if he could hear anything. Sure enough he could hear a gentle tapping sound.

"I can hear it too," he said. "I'll eat my sand eels and sit on the egg for a while. See if you can catch some sand eels, but don't be too long."

"All right," Mother Puffin replied. She waddled out of the burrow leaving Father Puffin sitting on the egg.

Father Puffin was just a little worried that the puffling might nibble through the shell of the egg and then peck him somewhere where he didn't want to be pecked. Every few minutes he moved off the egg to have another listen. As it happens, pufflings can take a day or two to hatch so he needn't have worried. Mother Puffin soon returned from her fishing trip.

"Back already!" Father Puffin said trying not to show that he was actually very pleased to see her.

"Yes," she replied. "How did you get on?"

"No trouble at all," he explained. "It was really quite easy."

"Good!" She said. "I'll take over again and stay here for the night. You can have another turn tomorrow."

"OK!" was Father Puffin's response. He was trying to sound enthusiastic but he'd already decided that he didn't want to be sitting on the egg when it hatched.

He made his way along the tunnel. It was actually very nice to see the daylight again, as it was extremely dark in the burrow and also very dusty. After a quick shake he flew out to sea, which is where most puffins spend the night. He'd decided fishing was a lot more fun than sitting on the egg waiting for it to hatch.

It was quite late when he returned to the burrow

the next morning and Mother Puffin was becoming a little worried that something might have happened to him.

"Where've you been?" she asked when he finally waddled into the nesting chamber.

"Catching sand eels is very tiring and I had to rest," he replied with a big yawn pretending he was tired.

"Rubbish, I know what you've been doing," Mother Puffin said. "You've been chatting to your mates. It's your turn to sit on the egg. I won't be too long. I'm certain you'll be fine while I'm away."

So much for Father Puffin's plans to keep away from the burrow! He examined the egg carefully as he swapped places with Mother Puffin. Very little seemed to have happened during the night. Father Puffin wasn't as worried as he'd been yesterday.

Mother Puffin left the burrow and soon found friends to chat to. She enjoyed being outside in the fresh air so she was in no hurry to return.

As the day wore on Father Puffin began to doze and was soon fast asleep. It wasn't long before he had good reason to wish he hadn't fallen asleep. The puffling inside the egg suddenly decided to get very busy. Father Puffin woke up with a start. Something was biting his bottom. The puffling had managed to pierce the shell of the egg and was now trying to get out, but Father Puffin's bottom was in the way.

"Ouch!" he exclaimed, as he leapt off the egg and banged his head on the roof of the burrow. "You little scoundrel!"

Mother Puffin just happened to be returning from her fishing when she heard Father Puffin's shout. She tried to waddle quickly along the tunnel to investigate. Waddling quickly isn't easy for puffins!

"What's the matter?" she asked as she arrived in the nesting chamber just in time to see Father Puffin trying to rub his head with one wing and his bottom with the other.

"I think that our puffling is very nearly ready to hatch," he replied. "Come and have a look!"

They swapped places and Mother Puffin peered at the egg.

"Oh, what a clever puffling!" she remarked. "It's done well!"

"Ouch!" he exclaimed, as he leapt off the egg and banged his head on the roof of the burrow. "You little scoundrel!"

Father Puffin was still recovering from the bang on his head and his sore bottom, so he found it difficult to agree with Mother Puffin.

"I think you'd better take over," he said. "I'm not very good at this."

"All right," she replied.

Father Puffin decided that sitting on hatching eggs was definitely not much fun! He waddled out of the burrow, had a quick shake and looked around to see what was going on. There were puffins coming and going everywhere. The hatching season was a busy time for all the puffins.

Father Puffin decided to fly to the fishing grounds to catch some more sand eels. He wanted to spend a few precious moments with his friends and see if any of them had had their bottoms pecked by pufflings. He realised that once his puffling was born, life would be hectic. There would be an extra mouth to feed!

Meanwhile, as the night wore on, the hole in the egg grew in size. Under the watchful eye of its mother the puffling was making steady progress. It would not be long before it hatched!

Mother Puffin tried not to get too excited, but she couldn't help herself. She was soon flapping her wings again and sure enough more sand filled the nesting chamber. This time she stopped quickly and brushed the sand away from the egg.

Gradually the puffling began to emerge. Suddenly there was a loud crack as the egg broke in two. Mother Puffin jumped and caused yet another shower of sand to fall from the roof of the burrow. As the dust cleared, Mother Puffin could see the curious creature that had emerged from the shell. Pufflings look nothing like their parents. They are fluffy bundles of grey fur with white tummies. They have a small beak like an ordinary bird. The brightly coloured bill grows later.

As this was the first time she had given birth to a puffling, Mother Puffin had never seen one before.

She took one look at the bundle of fur and rushed along the tunnel of the burrow shouting: "There's a strange creature in my burrow!"

She ran straight into Father Puffin who was returning to the burrow.

He wasn't very pleased!
"Calm down," he said. "What on earth is going on?"

"The egg broke," replied Mother Puffin trying not to panic, "and this strange creature popped out. It doesn't look anything like a puffin."

"Let me come and have a look," Father Puffin suggested.

He then waddled along the tunnel in front of Mother Puffin. When he got to the nesting chamber and saw the puffling, he looked at it carefully. He smiled and then turned to Mother Puffin.

"That's a perfectly healthy puffling," he said. "I've been chatting to some of my friends. They warned me that pufflings look very different from grown-up puffins."

Rather nervously Mother Puffin peeped out from behind Father Puffin and looked at the puffling. She studied it for a minute and then, very embarrassed at having made such a fuss, said: "Oh silly me! It's actually very cute."

She walked past Father Puffin into the nesting chamber. While she was looking at the front end of the puffling, Father Puffin decided to examine its back end. Mother Puffin wondered what he was doing.

"What are you looking at?" she asked.

"I'm trying to find out whether it's a boy or a girl," he replied. "We need to know if we're going to give our puffling a name."

The puffling didn't like being examined. It turned round and tried to peck Father Puffin.

"Oy!" said Father Puffin. "We'll have none of that!"

"Perhaps it's hungry," suggested Mother Puffin.

"Maybe," replied Father Puffin, "but it needn't peck me!"

"Well," said Mother Puffin. "I'm hungry. I'll go and get some food while you wait here and look after it."

"All in good time," Father Puffin replied. "I'm fairly certain it's a boy. Do you know what you'd like to call him?"

"Peter," suggested Mother Puffin.

"Right, Peter it is then," he agreed.

"Will you be all right looking after him?" she asked.

Father Puffin wasn't quite sure that he would be after what had happened so far!

"As long as it doesn't peck me again!" He said. "Is there anything that you want me to do while you're away?"

"You could tidy up some of the mess and then keep Peter warm," Mother Puffin suggested.

"OK," he replied. "I think I can manage that."

Mother Puffin waddled out of the burrow and disappeared. Father Puffin looked at Peter, and then at the pieces of eggshell littering the nest. He began to remove the larger pieces of eggshell to the back of the burrow.

Peter watched what was going on and decided to help. This wasn't a good idea! Peter grabbed a piece of eggshell but it was so big that it covered his face and he couldn't see where he was going. He walked straight into the wall. The piece of eggshell, which would have been quite easy to move when it was in one piece, had now been crushed into lots of pieces. This didn't please

Father Puffin, because it made clearing up the mess far more difficult.

"I know you're trying to help," said Father Puffin, "but it would be better if you sat down and kept out of trouble until your mother comes back."

Peter was very disappointed that he couldn't help. He sat in the nest and watched his father tidy up the mess. When he'd finished, Father Puffin nestled down beside Peter and they waited for Mother Puffin to return.

It wasn't long before they heard sounds at the end of the burrow. Mother Puffin soon appeared carrying four shiny sand eels in her bill. Peter didn't quite know what to make of them when they were placed on the ground in front of him.

"Go on!" said Mother Puffin. "Eat them! They're delicious!"

Peter looked at his mother and then at the sand eels, but wouldn't eat them.

"Watch!" said Mother Puffin.

She picked up one of the sand eels in her bill and it quickly disappeared down her throat. Peter was very hungry, so he tried to copy his mother. He grabbed one of the sand eels in his beak, but it was far too big for him. He tried shaking his head and twisting and turning but the sand eel just flapped about in his beak.

His parents started laughing.

Peter didn't think it was funny. He was hungry.
Father Puffin cut the sand eel in half and told Peter
to swallow it headfirst.

The sand eel disappeared very quickly down
Peter's throat.

"Don't worry, Peter!" said Father Puffin. "You'll
get the hang of it very quickly after a little
practice."

In fact Peter soon became an expert. He decided
that the sand eels were delicious. Pufflings are
very greedy and always want more. When
pufflings want something they make squeaking
noises. Peter spent a lot of time squeaking and kept
his parents very busy.

"All right," Mother Puffin would say when she
returned with sand eels, "We know what you want,
but you must be patient."

Father Puffin hadn't realised that pufflings could
eat so much. All this fishing was very tiring!

"I think I need to stay and watch Peter as he may
get up to mischief," he said on one occasion when
he'd returned to the burrow.

"You lazy old puffin!" Replied Mother Puffin. "Peter is quite capable of looking after himself. You need to help with the fishing!"

"What a pity!" was his response. "I was looking forward to a snooze."

Peter had noticed that when his parents greeted each other, they tapped their bills together several times very rapidly. This showed that the two puffins were pleased to see each other. Peter thought he'd like to do the same.

One day when Father Puffin returned to the burrow with some sand eels Peter decided to try the bill tapping. Father Puffin's bill was much larger than his tiny beak, so this was not a good idea. Peter banged his head when he tried to tap his father's bill.

Father Puffin suggested a slightly different way of greeting.

"It's much easier if you tap the end of my bill gently until your beak grows," he said. This worked very well. Peter did this each time one of his parents appeared with sand eels. It was also his way of saying thank you for the food.

Chapter Two: Adventures in the Burrow

Little by little Peter grew larger and larger. Of course the larger he grew, the more sand eels he needed, but his life was also becoming rather boring. He was either eating or sleeping. In his chamber it never got lighter or darker. It never got colder or hotter. Everything stayed the same. Mother Puffin had warned him not to wander out of the burrow.

"Peter," she had said, "whatever you do, you must stay in the burrow. Don't leave the tunnel. Outside there are very dangerous creatures who like to eat pufflings."

He hadn't really understood what she was talking about, but at the time he was quite happy and couldn't understand why he would want to go along the tunnel anyway.

As time went on, he felt more and more restless. He thought that there must be more to life than sleeping and eating.

One day he decided to do some exploring. Unfortunately pufflings can get themselves into trouble when they decide to do things they really shouldn't do.

He looked round the chamber and found a small twig. He had no idea where it had come from but he picked it up anyway. He then tried to eat it. Not only did it not taste very nice, but when he crunched it in his beak one end poked him in the eye.

He then noticed something sticking out of the sandy wall. Being very curious he grabbed it in his beak and pulled. Nothing happened. He thought he'd try again. This time he grabbed it very tightly and gave a big heave. It suddenly snapped and Peter ended up on his back with his feet in the air. He didn't like that so he decided to give up exploring and wait for the next lot of sand eels.

Over the next few days Peter became bored again. What could he do?

He'd explored every inch of his home and knew exactly where everything was. He looked carefully at the walls of his nesting chamber. Perhaps he could find something interesting by doing some digging in the chamber. He started digging with his feet. This was fun!

He'd made a little hole, but he'd found nothing interesting. He decided to carry on and dig a bigger hole.

Unfortunately Peter hadn't thought carefully about what he was doing. Very soon the area between the nesting chamber and the tunnel was almost completely blocked. It was Father Puffin who was next to visit with a large load of sand eels. Of course he'd no idea what Peter had been doing.

Father Puffin waddled straight into the pile of sand and went head-over-heels into the nesting chamber with sand eels flying in all directions.

"What on earth …?" He spluttered as he tried to stand up and collect all the sand eels that had fallen into the sand.

Peter looked at Father Puffin and realised that perhaps digging holes wasn't such a good idea. He and Father Puffin managed to put the sand back where it came from so that things would be back to normal when Mother Puffin arrived with the next lot of food.

"I know that there isn't much to do down here," said Father Puffin as he was on his way out, "but your mother and I are working very hard to make sure you have enough food. We've enough problems outside without you building an obstacle course in the tunnel."

Another failure! Peter needed another plan.

Although he'd been told not to go beyond the tunnel, he hadn't been told not to walk along it. So he decided to be brave and go exploring! He set off along the tunnel.

He walked a few paces round the corner. Suddenly he saw a bright light in the distance. Up till now Peter's whole world had been very dark. This was his first experience of daylight. He'd never seen anything like it before so he was very frightened and rushed back as quickly as he could to the safety of the nesting chamber.

It was another couple of days before he had the courage to explore the tunnel again. He set off carefully. This time he wasn't so frightened, but he was very puzzled when the light suddenly went out. He didn't realise that Mother Puffin had come into the tunnel with the next load of sand eels and had blocked out the light!

"Peter!" She said after she'd bumped into him and fallen flat on her face. "What are you doing? Go back to the nesting chamber. It's much easier for us if you just stay there and don't get in the way."

Peter wanted to tell her how bored he was, but decided there wasn't much she could do about it.

He soon realised that he could wander along the tunnel if he was careful. He knew that when the light went out, food was about to arrive and he needed to get back to the nesting chamber quickly. Peter thought that this was a fantastic discovery and it was a little game he could play.

In fact Peter became so bold that he wandered further and further along the tunnel each time it happened. Unfortunately one day he wandered too far. Mother Puffin met him quite near the entrance to the burrow and told him off again!

"Remember what I said," she warned. "Don't go outside the tunnel! It's very dangerous out there!"

Peter was very frustrated. He always seemed to get into trouble! He now had to think again. He wasn't very good at thinking!

He looked at the tunnel. What was at the end that was supposed to be so dangerous?

Although his parents had warned him not to go outside the tunnel, Peter thought that perhaps he could have a little peep if he was very careful. Surely it wasn't really that dangerous? Perhaps his parents were exaggerating when they said it was dangerous.

He waddled along the tunnel. As he approached the entrance, he began to hear a lot of noise. He stopped for a moment and then summoned up a little more courage. Little by little he moved towards the entrance. When he finally reached the mouth of the tunnel, he was amazed. It was a totally new experience.

Outside it was very bright and he could see all sorts of things that he'd never seen before. There was so much to see that he completely forgot his mother's warning and took a step beyond the entrance.

What happened next took place so quickly that it terrified Peter. As he was standing just outside the burrow, Peter suddenly became aware of what appeared to be a huge black shadow blocking out the sunlight. He sensed that something gigantic was hurtling towards him from the sky. He froze. He was very frightened and had no idea what to do. Just as it seemed that his short life might come to an end, Mother Puffin appeared from nowhere and threw herself between Peter and the huge black shadow.

Just as it seemed that his short life might come to an end, Mother Puffin appeared from nowhere and threw herself between Peter and the huge black shadow.

"Quick, get back inside!" she shouted to Peter.

At the sound of his mother's voice, Peter managed to forget his fear and disappear quickly into the burrow where he was safe. He was just in time! The huge black shadow was one of the gulls that love to eat little pufflings. These birds don't attack fully-grown puffins but are always on the prowl for naughty little pufflings who don't listen to their mother and father. With the arrival of Mother Puffin, the gull soared back into the sky looking for another target.

Mother Puffin waddled into the burrow after Peter. She was very relieved that he was safe, but she was also annoyed that he'd decided to go outside the tunnel despite her warnings.

"Peter," she said, "it was very stupid of you not to do as you were told. Outside the tunnel there are many birds who enjoy eating pufflings. You were very nearly breakfast for that gull. It was so lucky that I arrived when I did. Beyond the entrance to the tunnel things may appear to be exciting, but it is a very dangerous place for pufflings."

Peter was still shaking from his experience. He decided that in future he would listen to what his parents said. He thought that they seemed to know what they were talking about and were a lot wiser than a little puffling.

It wasn't long after this that strange things started happening to Peter. His fluffy coat, which is called "down", started to come off. Fluff was beginning to pile up in the burrow. Peter also noticed that his wings were growing. Flapping them in the burrow became more and more difficult as they became larger and larger. He had a feeling that there was about to be a big change in his life.

Mother Puffin knew exactly what was going on. She decided she needed to explain to Peter what would happen next.

"In a few days your father and I will be leaving you," she explained. "Soon afterwards, you must make your way to the end of the tunnel. I know I have told you not to go outside the tunnel, but this time you must. Just wait until it is dark."

Peter couldn't understand why his parents were going to leave him. Couldn't he go with them?

Mother Puffin knew what he was thinking.

"Pufflings have to learn to look after themselves," she continued, "All pufflings face this big test in life. When you get outside the tunnel, go to the edge of the cliff. Then jump! Don't stay on top of the cliff for too long as the gulls are sometimes still around at night. As I've told you, they like the taste of pufflings."

Peter was very puzzled, but Mother Puffin kept talking.

"From there you can jump and your wings will be strong enough to let you fly down to the water."

Peter was even more puzzled. What was water?

Mother Puffin again seemed to know what he was thinking and went on to explain.

"You'll find that the water is absolutely wonderful. Puffins really enjoy it. We swim in it, dive into it and fish in it. Just you wait and see. You'll love it."

Peter perked up a little. This seemed to be something nice to look forward to.

"Once you land on the water just dive underneath and swim," she continued. "Swimming will be very easy. Look at your feet. You have ready-made paddles."

Peter looked at his feet. He'd noticed that they'd become much bigger, which had made walking more difficult. He realised that they must be useful for this new adventure.

"When you land on the water, don't play around." Mother Puffin explained. "Swim away from the cliffs. Once you're out at sea, you can play around as much as you like!"

Peter didn't know what to think. There was so much to take in. He still didn't really understand why his parents couldn't stay with him.

"You have to do this on your own," Mother Puffin

said. "It has always been that way. You'll soon learn that puffins are really sea birds. You'll discover that you're a very good swimmer and you'll be able to catch your own food."

Peter quite liked the idea of catching food for himself. He could eat as much as he liked. He'd no idea that the sand eels might not be that easy to catch!

"You'll eventually come back here," Mother Puffin continued. "By that time you'll have grown into a strong and handsome puffin. You'll meet a beautiful female puffin and then have your own pufflings to look after."

Peter liked the idea of being strong and handsome but he had no idea where the beautiful female puffin would come from.

Peter had found it difficult to understand everything that his mother had told him. He decided to settle back into his routine and wait.

The next few days passed quickly. By now Peter had lost all his down. He'd been stretching his wings and trying to flap them. Although he didn't realise it, this was helping him get ready for his first flight. It hadn't been easy as he'd grown a lot and there wasn't much room in the burrow. He'd had to put up with clouds of dust, which had irritated him.

Eventually the day came when Mother Puffin and Father Puffin decided to leave. Father Puffin said good-bye to Peter first.

"Good-bye, Peter" he said.

They tapped bills for the last time. Peter had got a lot better at this, as his little beak had grown into a small bill.

"Remember to do exactly what you've been told once we've gone!" Father Puffin added. "Don't stay here for too long. All the other pufflings will be leaving in the next day or two. Good luck!"
Peter was getting butterflies in his tummy. He didn't like saying good-bye. He was beginning to feel very sad. He'd already decided that this time he'd do exactly what he'd been told!

Father Puffin also found it very difficult to say good-bye. He was well aware of the dangers that lie in store for all pufflings when they first head out to sea. He quickly turned round and waddled along the tunnel so that Mother Puffin could say her good-bye.

"Oh Peter!" she said, "I'll miss you. We'll see you again when you return. Once you get used to the sea, you'll realise that it's a much nicer place than this burrow. You'll be free!"

Peter had decided that he didn't particularly want to be free. He would have to think for himself.

Thinking for himself had always got him into trouble, so he was very worried.

There was a lot of bill-tapping as Mother Puffin said good-bye to her first puffling. Suddenly she turned around and was gone.

For the first time in his life Peter was truly all alone. He was very, very frightened. He looked around the nesting chamber that had been home for the two months of his short life. He wondered whether he'd ever see it again. Despite what his parents had said, he wasn't sure about the sea as he'd no idea what to expect. He'd never flown either. With his parents gone and no one to help him he felt very, very sad.

While he was sitting in the nesting chamber, Peter realised that there was no point in waiting any longer. Anyway there was no one to feed him, so he would soon be hungry! It was now or never!

He waddled slowly along the tunnel for the last time. It was gradually getting darker and darker outside. There was less and less noise as the gulls settled down for their night's sleep. Peter peeped out of the burrow.

All seemed to be quiet. He waddled forwards as fast as his little legs could carry him. He didn't have to go far. Suddenly he was aware of a big drop beneath him as he reached the edge of the cliff. He leapt over the edge flapping his wings as fast as he could.

This was the start of a new adventure.

Suddenly he was aware of a big drop beneath him as he reached the edge of the cliff. He leapt over the edge flapping his wings as fast as he could.

Chapter Three: New Friends at Sea

Peter hit the water with a splash! It was fff-rrrr-eezing!

But once he'd overcome the shock of the cold, he was very surprised at how wonderful it felt. He just wanted to splash around and enjoy himself. Then he remembered what he'd been told.

"I must get away from the cliffs as quickly as possible while it's still dark", he thought to himself.

He dived under the water and used his feet to start paddling.

"This is fun", he thought. His great big webbed feet made excellent paddles. He could whizz through the water.

Moments earlier he had been terrified as to what was going to happen. Now he was so happy! He felt as if he could swim forever. It was so much nicer than being stuck in that sandy burrow.

He popped up for a breath.

Under the water he dived again, whoosh!

Up again for another breath!

Under the water again with another whoosh!

He continued swimming for most of the night. The sea was fairly calm and he enjoyed bobbing up and down on the waves in between his dives.

Eventually it began to get light as night turned into day. He could still see the cliffs, but they seemed to be a long way away. He began to feel safe. He didn't realise that for little pufflings distances seem greater than they really are. He wasn't safe from the gulls just yet!

Peter was feeling quite hungry and there was no sign of anything to eat on top of the water.

"I wonder if there's anything down below," he thought.

He peered into the water under him, but there was no sign of anything interesting. He was about to dive under the water again when he heard a voice.

"Over here!" it said.

As he floated to the crest of the next wave he glanced in the direction of the voice. He saw two pufflings on top of another wave. He dived under the water and surfaced just beside them.

"Hi," said one of the pufflings, "I'm Holly and this is Ricky."

"Hello," Peter replied, "I'm Peter and I'm very hungry!"

"So are we!" Holly added.

Peter looked at the two pufflings. They looked exactly like him.

As it turned out, Holly was a very chatty puffling and Ricky seemed to be happy saying very little.

Peter remembered how pufflings were supposed to greet each other and so tried to tap bills with Holly. Because they were bobbing up and down on the waves, this was actually very difficult.

Every time they tried to tap each other's bill, a wave would lift one above the other so that they missed completely. They ended up tapping fresh air, which looked very funny!

"I don't think it's going to work." Holly said as they missed each other yet again.

"Never mind," Peter replied. "At least we tried."

Holly looked around and decided that they should keep swimming.

"I'm still not sure whether we're far enough from the cliffs," Holly said. "I think we ought to keep going. We can still look for food."

They dived under the waves together. While under the water, they looked for something to eat. They also kept an eye on each other to make sure that they didn't become separated. Holly surfaced after one swim looking very excited.

"I think I've spotted some sand eels," she exclaimed. "Follow me!"

The two pufflings followed Holly and sure enough there was quite a large school of sand eels drifting along quite slowly.

"Wonderful!" Peter thought. "Food! At last!"

He was very pleased he'd met Holly. She seemed to know what she was doing. He wasn't sure what to make of Ricky. He seemed happy just to follow along.

Peter had become very excited at the thought of being able to eat something.

He dived under the water to grab one of the sand eels. It hadn't occurred to him that the sand eels might not want to be caught. He was very surprised when the whole group scattered in all directions as he dived towards them.

"They moved!" he shouted when he surfaced.

"Of course they did," Holly replied. "You didn't expect them to stay still and let you eat them, did you?"

Peter thought about it and agreed with her. Peter began to realise that Holly was a very clever puffling. As Peter was not that bright, he thought it might be a good idea to make sure he stayed with her.

"How are we going to catch them?" he asked.

The three pufflings bobbed up and down on the waves for a minute or two. Meanwhile the sand eels had formed themselves into a big group again. Holly had a suggestion.

"I think we should dive at them at the same time but from slightly different directions. This might confuse them." She said.

"OK," Peter replied, "Let's have a go!"

The plan appeared to work but not completely.

The sand eels did seem to be confused, but so were the pufflings.

Peter nearly grabbed one of Ricky's feet while Ricky almost poked Holly in the eye. The three pufflings twisted and turned and did all they could, but with very little success.

Peter did manage to chop off a small piece of the tail of one sand eel but it appeared not to notice its loss. It just carried on swimming. Holly and Ricky had half a sand eel each as a result of catching the same one together and accidentally ripping it apart. All three pufflings surfaced feeling very frustrated and still very hungry.

"This is ridiculous," Peter complained. "How are we going to manage if we can't even catch our food?"

Peter and Ricky both looked at Holly hoping she would have another bright idea. She didn't let them down.

"We managed to confuse the sand eels," she said, "but because they seemed to scatter in all directions, we just snapped at the ones closest to us. We need a better plan!"

Peter agreed. He could feel his tummy rumbling. He needed food.

"When the sand eels scatter," Holly continued, "select one and race after it. We're much better swimmers and so this should work."

Peter thought about Holly's suggestion. He couldn't think of anything better and so he agreed to give it a go.

"Fine!" He said. "Let's try."

They dived again and this time they were far more

successful. The sand eels were quite easy to catch if the pufflings chased one at a time. Each of the pufflings had caught one when they next surfaced.

Most of Peter's had already disappeared down his throat because he was so hungry!

They dived again and this time they were far more successful.

After another couple of dives they'd become a lot more successful at catching their food. Once they'd finished eating, they decided it was time for a rest. They were very tired after all the fishing.

It was Ricky who spoke next, which was quite surprising as he hadn't said anything since Peter had met him.

"I'm still worried about the gulls," he said. "My parents told me about the puffling in the next door burrow. It wandered out of its burrow and was snatched by a big black gull."

Ricky's story reminded Peter of his own narrow escape and he felt rather embarrassed.

Peter looked at Ricky. He would learn that Ricky was a very serious puffling who only spoke when something really worried him.

"OK, then." It was Holly who came up with a plan yet again. "We'll have to take it in turns to keep watch. While two of us have a nap the other one will have to look out for gulls. Then we'll swop over. That should also make sure that we don't get separated."

Peter didn't think there was any danger of seeing gulls. He hadn't seen one for ages.

He did agree with Holly about becoming separated. He was beginning to like his new friends and didn't want to lose them.

Looking around the empty sky he asked her. "Do you really think there are gulls around?"

"Well," Holly replied, "I think it's better to be safe than sorry. Who's going to stay awake first?"

Peter realised that his friends were both looking at him and so he yawned.

"That's a good way to volunteer!" said Holly.

That hadn't been what Peter had hoped would happen. He was looking forward to a nap.

He realised he couldn't really complain and agreed to stay awake. It wasn't long before the other two pufflings were asleep and Peter was left to make sure that nothing happened.

Peter soon became bored as he'd been when he was in the burrow. He couldn't see any gulls.

"Why did I agree to this plan?" He thought, "I just want to have a snooze."

Of course becoming bored means losing interest! Losing interest means thinking of something else. What was Peter thinking about?

Sleep!

Gradually he felt more and more sleepy. Just as he was about to nod off, he suddenly noticed something out of the corner of his eye.

A gull had appeared from nowhere and was heading straight towards them.

"Quick!" He screamed to his friends. "Dive!"

The other two pufflings reacted very quickly to Peter's warning and all three dived together. They were only just in time. The gull lunged after them.

As the gull was not good at swimming under water, the pufflings managed to escape unharmed.

It had very nearly been a disaster.

All three pufflings stayed under water as long as they could. They wanted to make sure that the gull had disappeared before they surfaced. When they did eventually come up for air, there was no sign of their unwanted visitor.

Peter was again very embarrassed when he realised how stupid he'd been. He should have listened more carefully to his friends.

This was the second time he hadn't believed what he'd been told and nearly got himself killed. This time it was worse because he'd nearly got his friends killed as well.

"I'm very sorry," Peter said. "I didn't believe you when you said that there may be gulls about. I was half asleep. I don't know where the gull came from. One minute the sky was empty and the next minute it wasn't."

"Don't worry, Peter," Holly replied. "We all make mistakes, but we must be careful. Peter, you have a nap. Ricky and I'll stay awake and keep watch."

Peter was very glad to be able to have his long awaited sleep, as he was exhausted.

The next few days passed in much the same way. There were no more unwanted visitors.

When the three pufflings were not sleeping or eating, they had fun playing games. It was great fun diving into the waves and playing "chasey" under the water. It was actually Ricky who appeared to be the best at that. He seemed to be a slightly faster swimmer than Peter. Perhaps that was because he didn't eat as many sand eels as Peter!

By now the cliffs had completely disappeared from view. The three pufflings seemed to be in the middle of nowhere, but they stuck together. Every now and again they thought they'd spotted other pufflings when they were on the crest of a wave. Despite shouting, they had no luck in attracting their attention and so it was still a little group of three.

They hadn't really noticed but the size of the waves had increased. It also rained which didn't bother the pufflings. They could always avoid the rain by diving under the water.

It was after one particularly heavy shower of rain with some very strong winds that they realised that staying together was becoming more and more difficult.

"I think the time has come," Holly said, "to say our good-byes and split up."

Peter couldn't understand why they had to part.

"Why?" Peter asked. "We're very happy together."

"My parents told me that life at sea will get very difficult," Holly continued. "The best way to survive is to be prepared to be on your own."

Peter looked very confused. He couldn't remember his parents telling him that.

This time Ricky responded.

"My parents said the same," he added.

Peter decided that he ought to listen to them. The waves did seem to be getting bigger and bigger. It was becoming very difficult to stay together.

"OK." He said very reluctantly. "I know that one

day I'll go back to the cliffs. I hope we'll meet there again."

"Oh, I'm sure we will," Holly said.

They decided not to try any bill tapping. It had been a disaster when they had first tried. It would be hopeless now because the waves were that much bigger.

"Good luck, Peter!" Holly said. "We've had a great few days together. I look forward to seeing you again. Just be careful!"

"I will!" Peter replied. "Good-bye Holly, good-bye Ricky. Thanks for being good friends! See you again soon."

Ricky and Holly also said their good-byes. Not a moment too soon! Some particularly large waves appeared from nowhere and the three pufflings were swept apart.

Peter dived into one of the waves. When he surfaced neither of his friends was anywhere to be seen. For the second time in his very short life, Peter felt lonely and sad. He'd been really happy with Holly and Ricky. Now he was on his own again!

No one really knows why pufflings stay at sea for so long. No one is certain exactly where they go or what they do. During that time they learn to live on their own. They become really good at catching their food.

They also change from pufflings into beautiful puffins. Peter's bill grew and became brightly coloured. He developed a fine coat of feathers. His feet turned orange. They became really good paddles.

Eventually he felt this strong desire to go back to the cliffs.

Chapter Four: Return to the Cliffs

As if by magic Peter knew exactly how to get back to the cliffs. He wasn't that stupid after all!

When he'd left the cliffs as a puffling, it had been dark and very quiet. As he flew towards the cliffs as a puffin, he noticed that it was very noisy and also very busy. Not only puffins but all sorts of other birds seemed to be coming and going.

He glided towards the cliffs and found a place to land. He just hoped no one was watching. This was the first time he had landed on a firm surface. He didn't slow down quickly enough and went head over heels into a heather bush. He quickly brushed himself down and then heard a familiar voice.

"Well, if it isn't Peter," said the voice. "What a spectacular landing! It was very funny to watch."

He looked round to find Holly grinning at him. He was very embarrassed, but she looked very pretty now that she'd grown up and he was very pleased to see her.

"Don't worry," she added. "My first landing was nearly as bad. I arrived a few days ago and I saw Ricky yesterday."

Holly and Peter greeted each other by tapping bills, which was a lot easier now that they'd both grown up and weren't bouncing around on the waves. Holly took Peter to see Ricky. The three friends were really happy to be together again.

Holly seemed to know everything! She'd met quite a few of the puffins. She explained to Peter that she'd found out that he was related to her.

"Your mother and my father are sister and brother," she said. "That means that we're cousins. Would you like to see your mother?"

"That would be great!" Peter replied.

"Come along," Holly added. "I'll take you to see her. She's busy preparing for the arrival of another puffling."

Holly took Peter to his parents' burrow. He vaguely remembered it, but he'd never really seen it from the outside.

"Go and see her," Holly said.

Peter stood at the entrance to the burrow for a moment. He was a little nervous.

As he was standing there, his mother came out. She'd just been sitting on her new egg and was about to do some fishing.

She shook herself.

She then noticed Peter standing there. Because he'd changed so much, she didn't recognise him.

"Mother," he said a little sheepishly, "it's me, Peter."

She looked at him carefully.

"Well!" she replied. "How you've changed! What a handsome puffin!"

This embarrassed Peter, but the two puffins were really glad to see each other again. They tapped bills. She decided that fishing could wait for a minute.

She told Peter what had happened while he'd been away.

"You've got a sister," she said.

"Can I meet her?" Peter asked.

Mother Puffin smiled.

"She went to sea last year and hasn't come back yet," Mother Puffin explained.

He wondered if his sister was as clever as Holly.

"I want you to meet someone very special," Mother Puffin said.

"Who's that?" Peter asked.

"He's called Grandad," she continued. "He's probably the oldest puffin here. No one knows exactly how old he is. He's probably been alive for more than twenty-five years."

"Wow!" Peter replied. He had no idea how long twenty-five years was, but it sounded as if it was a long time.

"Come on," she said. "I'll take you to see him. He likes to meet the new puffins. He gives them very good advice."

Peter followed his mother a little way along the cliff top until they stopped outside a burrow that seemed to be in need of repair.

Mother Puffin poked her head inside.

"Cooee!" She called. "Is anyone at home?"

It wasn't long before a puffin with a magnificent bill waddled out of the burrow. As puffins get older, their bills grow larger and larger.

"Wow!" Peter thought. "That bill is quite something!"

Grandad was a little unsteady on his feet, but was clearly a very important puffin.

"Grandad," Mother Puffin said. "This is Peter. He's my son."

"Welcome, my boy," Grandad replied.

He was always happy to meet another member of his enormous family.

He tapped bills with Peter. Grandad's bill was so big that it nearly knocked poor Peter off his feet.

"Most of the puffins call me Grandad," he continued, "as I think I'm related to just about everyone."

Peter was lost for words, which was unusual for Peter! He still couldn't take his eyes off the enormous bill, which had nearly knocked him over.

"If you come back tomorrow when you've had a good look round, I'll tell you a few things about puffins." He added. "I like to make sure that all my young relations know how to take care of themselves."

"I certainly will," Peter replied.

Peter and his mother chatted for a while before she decided she needed to go fishing.

"I have an egg that needs looking after," she said eventually. "I won't be able to spend time with you, so take care and enjoy yourself."

She said good-bye to him, leaving him to go and find Holly and Ricky.

"I'd like to have a look round," Peter said when he'd found his friends. "Do you want to come?"

"Why not?" Holly replied.

The three friends set off to do some exploring. They didn't get far before Peter discovered that this was quite difficult. His great big orange feet were not designed for walking. He tripped over a clump of heather and fell flat on his face.

"Perhaps this isn't such a good idea!" he muttered trying to remove bits of heather from his wings.

They'd just turned round when a shout came from one of the other puffins.

"Look out! Take cover!"

Peter looked up and saw a very wobbly Grandad approaching the cliff top rather like an out-of-control aircraft. Grandad's flying skills had clearly got worse as he'd got older. He seemed to have little control over where and how he landed.

Puffins ran in all directions to avoid being flattened by Grandad. More by luck than good judgement Grandad found a soft place to crash-land. There was a flurry of feathers and an explosion of sand as he belly-flopped on to the clifftop.

Puffins ran in all directions to avoid being flattened by Grandad.

"Made it," he sighed as he brushed himself down and waddled towards his burrow. Peter and his friends found the event rather amusing, but at the same time they felt very sorry for Grandad as he obviously found flying very tricky.

Peter's first day back on the clifftop had been very tiring but quite an experience.

"How different from all those days at sea!" He thought to himself.

As the sun was beginning to set, he decided that a rest might be a good idea. Puffins prefer to sleep on the sea, as it keeps them away from hungry creatures on land that might just take advantage of a puffin sleeping on the clifftop.

Peter joined a group of puffins on the water and was soon fast asleep.

Next day once the sun had started to rise, Peter began to realise he was very hungry. What a surprise! He flew off in search of breakfast. It wasn't long before he'd found some sand eels.

Once back on the cliff top, he decided to visit Grandad. Peter reached the burrow just as Grandad emerged from the tunnel. Some of the older puffins seem to prefer sleeping in their burrows.

"Good morning Grandad!" Peter said. "Have you had a bit of a lie-in?"

"When you get to my age, there's no need to hurry," he replied. "I've plenty of time to do what I have to do."

"Yesterday you told me that there were things I should know," Peter said.

"Very true," Grandad replied.

He stretched himself and had a shake.

"There are many different types of birds living here," Grandad continued. "Most of them take no notice of each other. We all have things to do and so we mind our own business."

"Thank goodness for that!" Peter thought.

"However, you do have to watch out for some of them," Grandad explained.

"Why is there always a catch?" Peter wondered. He was hoping not to have to worry about dangers.

Grandad stopped talking and looked carefully into the sky. He soon spied what he was looking for.

"There!" he said. "Can you see that large gull with a black back?"

"Yes," Peter replied as he watched a very large gull flying effortlessly through the air.

"Gulls are usually only a threat to pufflings which is why parents worry about their youngsters, but that one there will attack grown-up puffins." He said. "It looks harmless, but those birds will attack a puffin if it's flying on its own or seems to be struggling."

Peter looked at the bird as it continued to fly lazily along the edge of the cliffs. It didn't seem to be a threat, but Peter felt certain Grandad knew what he was talking about.

"You also need to be careful when you bring back sand eels for your beautiful female puffin or a young puffling," Grandad continued.

Peter hadn't even thought about finding a beautiful female puffin let alone having his own puffling.

"I wonder what I have to do to find a beautiful female puffin?" He thought.

He didn't think for too long, because he realised he should be listening to Grandad.

"There are some birds that will attack you when you have a mouthful of sand eels," he said. "It is best just to drop the sand eels and fly away. These birds are bigger than you. You could get into trouble if you do anything else."

Peter looked at Grandad who smiled.

"Some of the birds aren't very good at fishing," Grandad explained, "and so they let us do all the hard work and then they steal what we've caught."

This seemed most unfair to Peter.

Grandad seemed to know what Peter was thinking.

"You have to learn, Peter, that the world isn't fair," Grandad replied. "Some birds are stronger and more powerful than others, so they take advantage of the ones who are smaller and weaker."

"Will I meet any other creatures on the cliffs?" Peter asked.

"Oh yes," Grandad replied. "Wait until you see creatures called 'people', they are unlike anything you have seen so far."

"Are people bigger than gulls?" Peter asked.

Grandad chuckled. "Yes, much bigger!"

"It must be very frightening seeing one of them flying around," Peter said.

Grandad laughed again. "People can't fly!"

Peter was astonished. He hadn't seen anything on the cliffs that couldn't fly.

"There is also one creature that can be a danger

when you're on the water," Grandad added looking at Peter.

"Oh?" Peter replied but he was still thinking about creatures on the cliffs that couldn't fly. "Do people swim? Are they better at swimming than we are?"

Grandad smiled.

"No, Peter," Grandad said. "I've never seen people swimming. I've only ever seen them walking along paths on top of the cliffs."

Peter couldn't understand. This was far too difficult for him. Large creatures that couldn't fly and may not be able to swim! These seemed to be very strange creatures!

"One day I'll tell you all about people," Grandad replied. "You needn't worry about them at the moment. I want to tell you about the one animal that can be a worry when you're in the water."

Peter had thought that he was quite safe on the water.

"You have to be careful of seals at this time of year," Grandad replied. "They are large animals that live along the shoreline. Being very good swimmers they spend a lot of time in the water. Their youngsters seem to like a juicy piece of puffin."

Peter looked worried.

"It's not all bad news," Grandad continued. "Seals will usually only attack puffins when a puffin is on its own. That's why puffins tend to keep together. Also the seals are only a threat for a short time when the young seals are growing very quickly and need lots of food."

Peter was learning a lot about the joys and dangers of being a puffin. He was very grateful to Grandad for all the information. He wondered whether all the other puffins knew about the dangers that seemed to lurk round every corner.

"Now it's time for me to go and do some fishing." Grandad said. "Do you mind giving me a helping hand? I find it a little difficult taking off. A gentle shove will do."

Rather reluctantly Peter gave Grandad a push off the edge of the cliff and peered after him anxiously as he disappeared at an alarming rate towards the water. He needn't have worried as Grandad's wings were soon flapping vigorously.

Peter wandered along the cliff top and thought about Grandad's advice. It did seem a strange world. He was beginning to wonder why he'd come back to the colony as there seemed to be all sorts of dangers and he'd been very happy on the water.

He decided to spend some time standing on the cliff top taking in what was going on around him. He did remember to keep an eye out for the nasty gulls!

It wasn't too long before Grandad was on his way back from his fishing.

The now familiar cry of "look out!" warned Peter that he ought to watch out. He soon spotted poor Grandad seemingly totally out of control heading in the general direction of the cliff top with puffins scrambling for cover ready for another crash-landing.

Peter waddled over to where he thought Grandad had landed, but there was no sign of him.

"He must be here somewhere," Peter thought.

He peered over the edge of the cliff and saw two legs that certainly belonged to a puffin flapping in the air. From underneath the legs came some muffled cries for help. Grandad had misjudged his landing in spectacular fashion.

He had ended up stuck in a gull's nest in a gap in the rocky cliff. The surprised gull had been forced to leave her nest in a hurry and was flapping around squawking at the upside-down puffin.

Peter dropped down beside Grandad and managed to lever the poor old puffin out of his rocky landing place. Grandad was very grateful.

"Thank you, Peter," he said. "Landing on the cliff tops is not for oldies like me. My sense of judgement has got worse and worse over the last few years."

"You must be careful," Peter replied. "I'm sure that upside-down puffins make easy targets for some of those nasty birds you were telling me about earlier."

"I know, Peter," Grandad agreed. "This'll be the last season that I come to land. Grandma and I have been coming here for many years. We'd go our separate ways at the end of each year. Somehow we'd always find our way back the following year to the same burrow to bring up another puffling."

Peter was now beginning to realise that the real reason for coming back to the cliffs was to have pufflings. He'd been wondering why he'd come back. Now he knew!

Grandad was still speaking.

"This is the first time that Grandma hasn't turned up," he said sadly. "I think something must have happened to her during the winter or else she'd definitely be here. I'm afraid she may have died during one of the winter storms."

They wandered back to the burrow in silence. Peter said nothing, as he realised that the two puffins must have been very fond of each other. Without her Grandad would be feeling very lonely. When they reached the burrow Grandad spoke again.

"Grandma and I built this burrow together many years ago and it's not very nice here without her. It'll not be long before I fly out to sea for the last time. Along with all puffins I've always enjoyed being at sea where we're free to do what we like."

Peter agreed. He'd enjoyed being at sea, but he felt very sorry for Grandad. He'd obviously had a happy life but was now very sad being here without Grandma.

"By the way Peter," Grandad remarked. "As I won't be coming back next year, you're welcome to take over my burrow. You and some lovely female puffin can use it year after year to bring up your own pufflings."

Again there was this talk of finding a female puffin and having pufflings. Peter didn't understand how it happened.

"Thank you very much," Peter replied. "That's very kind of you, but where will I find this wonderful puffin to share the burrow with me?"

"Don't you worry about that," Grandad said.

"These things just happen. You'll know when the time is right. It could be this year or it may be next year."

"How will I know?" Peter thought to himself. This was very confusing for a young puffin.

"Anyway the burrow is in need of some urgent repairs as parts of the tunnel have collapsed," Grandad continued. "You'll need to do some digging. Mysterious things seem to happen to burrows during the winter while we're away."

"I'm sure it's a lot easier to take over a burrow that needs repairing, rather than having to build one from nothing," Peter remarked.

"Yes, that's true," Grandad replied with a yawn. "Time for a snooze I think. We'll have a chat again soon."

"Good-bye Grandad," Peter said, "and thank-you for all the advice. You'll let me know when you decide to fly back to sea, won't you?"

"Don't worry," he replied. "I won't leave without saying good-bye."

Peter had enjoyed his time with Grandad. He thought carefully about everything that he'd been told. He was certainly looking forward to meeting a lovely female puffin. That sounded great! Someone like Holly perhaps!

He spent the rest of the day with his friends before flying out to sea as usual for his night on the water. He was beginning to understand why the puffins spend so much time together and seem to enjoy each other's company.

He flew back to the cliff top next morning in time to hear sounds of a great commotion. He wandered over along the cliff top to see what was happening. Holly was already there.

"What's going on?" Peter asked.

"One of the younger puffins has wandered into another puffin's burrow," Holly replied. "The owner didn't like it and has become very angry."

"It does seem to be very serious," Peter remarked.

Sure enough there were feathers flying in all directions, as the two puffins attacked each other with their bills. They cart wheeled over the turf, bouncing over burrows that happened to be in their path.

Puffins scattered as the two fighting puffins continued to tumble towards the cliff-edge. Although quite an audience had gathered to watch what was going on, no one seemed to be worried as to what might happen to either of the two puffins.

As the two puffins rolled nearer and nearer the

edge, Peter became more and more anxious. He felt certain that something terrible was going to happen.

As it turned out the two puffins bounced over the edge of the cliff and then separated. The angry puffin chased the other one out to sea. Peter soon lost sight of them, but neither seemed to have been harmed.

Peter was quite shocked.

"I didn't realise that puffins could get so angry," Peter remarked.

"I think we ought to make sure that we don't upset any of the grown-ups, especially while they're bringing up young pufflings," Holly replied. "We need to keep out of burrows that are already occupied."

"I agree," Peter replied. "I don't want to get into any fights."

Holly smiled. "Peter, I can't imagine you fighting anyone."

Peter looked at Holly. She really was a very good friend.

"I've been thinking of trying to find an empty burrow for myself," Holly went on. "It's a lot of work having to dig a new one. Peter, I think you might need to do the same."

Peter told Holly about Grandad's offer.

"What a lucky puffin!" Holly replied. "He's very kind and that'll save you a lot of trouble."

Peter had begun to realise just how lucky he was. Over the next few days he settled into a routine before his next adventure.

Chapter Five: New Adventures

Peter had met another puffin called Simon. Simon was a lot more adventurous than Peter. One day they were chatting.

"Have you ever seen any people?" Peter asked.

"Yes," Simon replied. "I have."

"Are they dangerous?" Peter said.

"The ones I've seen don't seem to be dangerous," Simon continued. "They're rather strange."

"Can we see some?" Peter asked.

"I don't see why not," Simon said. "We'll have to fly along the cliffs a bit, because people don't seem to come to this area."

"OK," Peter replied.

"People tend to come out when the weather is fine," Simon remarked.

He looked up at the sky. There were some rain clouds about, but otherwise it was a sunny day.

"I'm sure we can find some," he continued. "Are you ready?"

"Yes!" Peter replied.

Peter was quite excited. Ever since Grandad had told him that people were big creatures that couldn't fly and might not be able to swim, he'd wanted to see some.

Simon seemed certain that people weren't dangerous and so Peter was looking forward to this adventure.

They flew along the cliffs and then landed in an area that Peter had never visited.

"Over there!" Simon said pointing at a group of people walking along a path.

Peter looked. He was amazed. He'd seen nothing like this before.

"What are they doing?" He asked.

"They always seem to walk along that path," Simon explained. "When they get nearer the cliffs they wander all over the place."

"Perhaps they're looking for food," Peter suggested.

"I don't think so," Simon replied. "When they see puffins, they get very excited."

"What do they do next?" Peter asked.

"They usually stop and point things at us," Simon explained. "Then they move on. It's really very strange."

Peter didn't understand.

"Why do they point things at us?" Peter asked. He seemed to be asking a lot of questions and hoped that Simon didn't mind.

"I've no idea!" He replied. "None of the puffins I've asked seem to know. It's a mystery. That's why I think people are strange."

What the puffins didn't know was that people point cameras at them to take photos!

Peter watched the people walking along the path. They were different shapes and sizes, some thin, some fat, some tall and some short. Also they were different colours. Some were multi-coloured!

Peter continued to ask more questions.

"Why are they different colours?" He asked.

"I'm not sure," Simon replied. "Sometimes they change colour!"

Peter couldn't understand how anything could change colour. He also noticed that the people had humps on their backs.

"What are those humps on their backs?" he asked.

"The people can take the humps off their backs," Simon explained. "Inside them the people have things that make them change colour. They usually change colour when it rains or when it gets hot."

Peter thought about this. He wondered what would happen if he changed colour every time it rained.

They didn't have long to wait before it did actually start raining. Sure enough the people stopped walking. They took off their humps. They took something out of their humps and then they changed colour.

The people put their humps back on and carried on walking.

"Do they change colour again when it stops raining?" Peter asked.

"Yes, they do," Simon said.

Peter was a little embarrassed at having to ask so many questions, but he was so amazed at what was going on.

The people were getting much closer. Peter was beginning to become a little anxious.

"Are you sure it's safe to stay here?" He asked.

"Quite sure," Simon replied.

Peter was relieved. He enjoyed watching the people. They seemed to be so very strange. Just then one of the people seemed to dive into a heather bush. When it got up again it made some very strange noises, quite unlike anything Peter had heard before!

"What's that one doing?" Another question!

"I think it's rather annoyed!" Simon replied. "People tend to make loud noises when they fall over."

"I wonder why?" Peter thought. "Puffins are always falling over and they don't make a noise."

"Perhaps that one has found something to eat in the heather bush and is telling his friends," Peter suggested.

"I don't think so," Simon said. "The humans keep their food in their humps."

"That's amazing!" Peter replied. "I wish we had humps to store food. We could catch lots of sand eels in one go and then eat them whenever we were hungry."

Peter and Simon continued watching the people. A few minutes later something else happened.

One of the people had slipped over while going down a steep bit of the path. It had fallen on its hump and was lying on its back waving its arms and legs in the air. At the same time it was making a noise.

Peter thought it looked rather funny. One of the other people then helped it back on its feet.

Peter remembered when he had had to help Grandad out of the gull's nest. People could behave just like puffins!

A little later it stopped raining. The people also stopped walking. They sat down.

They took off their humps and changed colour again. They also took things out of their humps and started eating them.

Peter was beginning to think that humans were quite clever as well as being quite strange.

The people got up and put their humps back on. Suddenly one of them made a noise and pointed towards Simon and Peter.

"What's happening?" Peter asked.

"I think we've been spotted." Simon replied. "If they get too close, we'll just fly away. For the moment, just hide behind this heather bush."

There was more noise from the people. One of them started walking towards the two puffins. Peter and Simon were just about to fly off when something else very strange happened.

The one walking had gone too close to a bird that was sitting on its nest. The bird was very angry. It dive-bombed the walker, dropping a large pooh on its head. The walker was obviously very annoyed and made another noise.

The other people seemed to think it was very funny!

Simon and Peter didn't like all the noise and so they decided to stay behind the heather bush. The people walked past them and continued along the path.

The two puffins popped out from behind the bush. The people were disappearing from view.

"That was very strange!" Peter said. "The people didn't point anything at us."

"They usually do," Simon replied. "If we wander along the cliff top, we might see some more."

Peter was in no hurry to go back.

"OK!" He said.

He was feeling quite bold and thought that people

were very peculiar creatures. The two puffins didn't have far to go before they spotted two more people sitting on two large rocks.

"Stop!" Simon said to Peter.

Peter stopped.

"We'll wait behind these heather bushes and see what happens," Simon continued.

They each hid behind a heather bush and waited.

Both the people seemed to be very big. One had something very large on its head, which covered most of its face. The other had a much smaller thing on its head. They had humps like the other people. Peter noticed that one had two large bulges on its front.

"Simon?" Peter asked.

"Yes," Simon answered.

"Why does one of the people have two large bulges on its front?" He said.

"I've noticed that before," Simon replied. "It's a bit of a mystery."

"More mysteries!" Peter thought.

It was quite warm now that the rain had stopped.

The people were wiping their faces with something. As they were very close to these people, Peter could see that they had very red faces. He wondered if all people had very red faces.

He decided to pop his head round the edge of the heather bush to get a better look.

He was immediately spotted by one of the people, in fact the one with the two bulges. It appeared to be so surprised that it gave a little shriek.

Two things happened.

Peter darted behind the bush.

The other one of the two people got up from where it was sitting.

To Simon and Peter it looked enormous. They hadn't been that close to people before and so hadn't realised they could be so big.

"I'm scared!" Peter said.

"Time to go!" Simon replied.

Simon nipped out from behind the bush and quickly flew off.

As Peter was about to fly away, he turned round. He saw that something was being pointed at him.

He was immediately spotted by one of the people, in fact the one with the two bulges.

He knew he wasn't supposed to be frightened, but he was!

What do puffins do when they're frightened? Like many other creatures they do a poo!

Just as Peter did his poo, he heard a click from

behind him.

He didn't realise but his timing was perfect! One of the people had taken a photo of Peter doing a poo!

The other one seemed to think this was very funny, but Peter didn't stay to find out what might happen next.

He quickly took off and followed Simon back to their part of the cliff top.

They landed almost together.

"You were right," Peter said to Simon. "One of the people pointed something at me just before I flew off. It seemed to make a noise but nothing else happened."

"Perhaps we'll never know why people point things at us." Simon replied. "I hope you enjoyed the day."

"Yes," Peter replied. "Very much, thank you."

Peter decided to visit Grandad to find out what he knew about people. When Peter reached the burrow, he found Grandad staring out to sea.

"Why do people point things at puffins?" Peter asked.

Grandad shook his head.

"No one seems to know," he said. "People come here every year. They get as close as they can to puffins. Then they point things at us and go away."

"How strange!" Peter replied. "Do people ever harm puffins?"

"I've never met any people who harm puffins," he replied. "One year, however, when I was at sea, I met a puffin who belonged to a group who lived a long way from here. He was telling me that people can harm puffins."

Peter wondered why people wanted to harm puffins.

"The people we meet seem to get very excited when they see us," Grandad continued. "I don't know why. We're only puffins!"

Peter couldn't understand why either.

"Perhaps it's because we're very special," Peter said.

Grandad just looked at him and smiled. Peter then left Grandad and wandered along the cliff.

Peter was thinking about his conversation with Grandad and not looking where he was going. He walked straight into a puffin that was busy cleaning itself.

"Sorry!" He said as the poor puffin struggled to stop itself falling over.

"Not to worry!" The puffin replied. "I shouldn't have been standing in the path."

Peter looked at the puffin and started to get goose bumps (or should we say puffin bumps!).

"What's your name?" Peter asked.

"Ellie!" It replied.

"A female puffin!" Peter thought, "and a very pretty one!"

To Peter she looked gorgeous. She was a bit smaller than many of the other puffins, but there was something about her that Peter found really wonderful.

"I don't think I've seen you before," Peter said.

"No, you probably haven't," Ellie replied. "I've only been here a few days."

"Come on then," Peter said. "I'll show you round!"

"I'm actually quite hungry," Ellie replied.

"So am I!" Peter said. "I've had a busy day. I'll tell

you all about it."

They flew out to sea in search of sand eels. Peter was keen to impress his new friend.

"You sit on the water," he said. "I'll go and find some food."

"That's very kind," Ellie replied. "Thank you!"

It wasn't long before Peter had enough sand eels for both of them.

Peter told Ellie about his adventures with the people. She listened very carefully. She was very impressed.

"What an exciting life you have!" She said.

After some more chatting, they settled down for the night with a large group of puffins.

"Is this what Grandad meant when he told me I would find a special female puffin?" Peter thought as he drifted off to sleep. He felt so very, very happy.

Over the next few days Peter and Ellie spent more and more time with each other. Peter thought she was gorgeous and was very protective of her in front of his other friends. In turn Ellie had grown very fond of Peter.

Little by little, Peter began to notice that the summer was ending. He was starting to feel restless. He realised that he would soon have to go back to sea for the winter.

Peter decided he needed to discuss this with Ellie. Because she was smaller than most of the puffins, Ellie would sometimes have difficulty flying, particularly when the wind was very strong. This worried Peter.

The next day it was blowing a gale. Ellie found it difficult to stay upright.

"I'm finding it very difficult in this wind," she said to Peter.

Peter decided he needed to show her that the wind wasn't as strong as she thought.

"Come on," he replied. "It's not that bad!"

He launched himself into the air, only to make a real fool of himself. He was caught by a gust of wind that turned him upside-down. He was then whirled round and round. Despite trying to steady himself using his wings, he lost control completely and landed upside-down in a heather bush.

"Oh! Peter," Ellie exclaimed. "You are funny!"

Peter was very embarrassed.

"That wasn't supposed to happen!" He said when he'd got back to his feet.

The wind was very strong and he decided that it was time to talk to Ellie about returning to sea.

"Ellie," he said trying to be serious, "I'm beginning to feel that it's nearly time to fly out to sea for the winter. That may well mean that we'll not be able to stay together."

"I know, Peter," Ellie replied. "I was thinking about it as well. I know we can't stay here through the winter. We have to leave."

"I'm worried about you," Peter said. "I know you struggle in the wind."

"I've managed before," Ellie replied.

"You must be careful!" Peter said.

"I will!" Ellie answered sighing gently. "Anyway I want to come back next year and see you again."

Peter smiled. "I want to see you as well."

Peter looked around him. He realised that some of the puffins had already left. There weren't as many on the clifftop as there had been a few days ago.

He decided they ought to do some fishing. It would help if they weren't hungry when they flew out to sea. Despite the wind they both managed a successful takeoff.

Finding sand eels had become more difficult as the summer had passed, so they had to go quite a way. They eventually found a group of puffins fishing and so they joined them.

While they were fishing it was easy for the puffins to become separated so, when Peter had finished, he had to search for Ellie. She was some way away. By the time Peter had found her, all the other puffins had taken off for the shelter of the clifftop.

The wind had got stronger and was coming from one side. Puffins prefer flying with the wind behind them. Peter was now becoming very concerned. Not only were the two of them on their own, but Ellie was going to find the wind extremely difficult.

"Come on Ellie!" Peter said. "We must go."

"OK," she replied as they took off together, "I needed a little rest."

It wasn't long before Peter noticed that Ellie was really struggling.

"Peter!" She said. "I'm sorry but I need a rest!"

"OK," he replied, "but we can't stay on the water

for too long. It isn't safe. There are still some nasty gulls about."

"I know, but I'm so tired," Ellie explained.

They landed on the water but it wasn't long before Peter realised that they'd been spotted. There was a large gull circling above them waiting to pounce.

"Ellie," he said. "We're in real danger. We must go!"

"Oh! Peter," she repeated, "I'm so tired!"

"Come on!" Peter urged. "The cliffs aren't that far away. We must try to get to safety quickly!"

The two puffins took off again and headed towards the cliffs.

The gull wasn't stupid. It knew which of the two puffins was struggling. Peter also realised that the gull had its eyes on Ellie.

"Come on!" He screamed at Ellie. "You must fly faster! We're being chased!"

"I can't!" she protested. "I'm exhausted!

Those were the last words that she uttered. In an instant the gull had folded its wings and swooped. It plucked Ellie out of the sky and carried her off.

One moment Ellie had been flying with Peter, the next she was gone and there was nothing he could do. Peter landed on the clifftop and looked back. The gull had disappeared with Ellie. Peter would never see her again.

Peter was so upset.

He didn't know what to do, so he decided to go and find Grandad.

When he arrived at the burrow, Grandad was having a snooze.

"Grandad!" Peter said.

Grandad woke up and saw Peter.

"Oh!" he said looking at Peter. "I was about to come looking for you. I've decided its time to leave."

"Ellie's gone," Peter continued.

"What do you mean, gone?" Grandad asked.

"A seagull ......" Peter couldn't say any more.

"Oh!" Grandad replied. "I see!"

After a long pause, Grandad continued. "Peter, I'm very, very sorry. I know you liked her a lot. Life is hard and at times very unfair."

"Ellie was very special," Peter explained. "Why did it have to happen to her?"

Grandad paused again.

"I don't know," he said very slowly. "These things happen and no one knows why. There's only one thing to do."

"What's that?" Peter asked.

"Go!" Grandad replied. "It's time for you to leave and fly out to sea."

"Ellie and I had been talking about that," Peter explained.

"You'll never forget Ellie," Grandad said, "but you'll come back next year and you'll find another special female puffin. You'll like her as much as you've liked Ellie."

Peter was not so sure. Grandad was usually right, but Peter thought that he was wrong this time.

"When you return," Grandad continued, "make sure you come back to this burrow. I've tried to tidy it up a bit. It's been a wonderful home to Grandma and me for many years so take good care of it."

"Thank you Grandad," Peter replied. "I'm really

grateful for all your help, but I can't think of anything else but Ellie at the moment."

"You'll feel better once you're out at sea," Grandad explained. "Just be careful and don't do anything foolish."
Peter looked at Grandad. He somehow knew that he would never see him again.

"Good-bye, Grandad," he said.

"Good-bye, Peter," Grandad replied. "Good luck! You will be happy one day, I know!"

Those were the last words that Grandad said to Peter.

They tapped bills.

Peter turned round and took off. He soared into the sky. He did a loop, took one final look at Grandad standing outside his burrow and then flew out to sea.

Peter turned round and took off.

Chapter Six: A Challenge

The winter at sea passed very quickly. By spring Peter was feeling the urge to return to land. He couldn't understand why he had this strong feeling. He'd been so unhappy when he'd left.

He somehow knew that he was flying in the right direction. Sure enough he soon spotted the familiar clifftops. He got closer and closer, eventually making a safe landing. He shook himself and was about to set off in the direction of Grandad's burrow when he spotted Holly and Ricky.

"Hello, Holly," Peter said. "Have you been back long?"

"Hello, Peter," Holly replied. "No, Ricky and I arrived yesterday."

"You came back together?" Peter asked.

"Yes," Holly replied a little embarrassed. "We managed to spend the winter together, although it was quite difficult at times."

"That was very clever," Peter said. "I suppose you know what happened to Ellie just before I left?"

"Yes, we were very sad." Holly explained. "You must find another female puffin as soon as possible."

"I don't really know where to start," Peter said. "It's going to be very difficult to find a puffin as wonderful as Ellie."

"Well," Holly replied with a smile. "I happen to know of a very beautiful puffin who's been here for only a short while but has already managed to attract a lot of interest from other male puffins. Her name is Sally. We'll wander along the clifftop and see if we can find her. She'll probably be surrounded by puffins trying to attract her attention."

"Wow!" Peter replied. "This sounds like a challenge!"

They wandered along the clifftop. It wasn't long before they spotted a beautiful female puffin surrounded by several interested males, although one particularly large puffin seemed to be keeping the rest at a distance.

"She's certainly very beautiful!" he said. "How can I get near her?"

"Why don't you take her a present?" Holly suggested.

"Wonderful idea!" Peter replied and looked round to see what he could find.

There was quite a large gull's feather nearby and

he thought this would be ideal. He picked it up in his bill and set off towards the beautiful puffin. The feather was very large. Because there was a gusty wind, Peter found that waddling along the cliff top with a large feather in his mouth was actually very difficult.

The feather acted as a sail and several times Peter nearly fell over trying to keep his balance. Eventually he reached the beautiful puffin.

Peter then had to make his way with his present through the group of adoring puffins. He managed to poke one in the eye and another in its bottom, so by the time he reached Sally he wasn't very popular.

At last he got there. Just as he was about to give Sally his present, the feather tickled Peter's nose. Peter sneezed. It was such a big sneeze that it blew Sally over.

As he sneezed, Peter let go of the feather and it was blown away by a gust of wind.

What a disaster! The present was gone! The beautiful puffin was lying on the ground! Not a good start!

The large puffin, that had been protecting Sally, waddled up to Peter.

Just as he was about to give Sally his present, the feather tickled Peter's nose. Peter sneezed. It was such a big sneeze that it blew Sally over.

"Push off!" He said giving Peter a shove.

Peter didn't like the look of this puffin. He was very big and seemed to be very aggressive.

Sally was quite impressed that Peter had decided to bring her a present.

"That was kind of you," she said when she got back to her feet.

"Hi!" Peter replied trying to hide his embarrassment. "I'm sorry about that. I thought you might like a present. It all went rather wrong. My name's Peter."

"Hello," the beautiful puffin replied. "I'm Sally."

"She is certainly very beautiful!" Peter thought.

The large male puffin didn't like Sally talking to Peter. He'd already decided that Sally was going to be his and no one else's! He thought he'd better do something quickly.

"So your name's Peter," he said threateningly. "Well my name's Greg and I haven't any time for puffins making fools of themselves. I suggest you go back to where you came from."

Peter was rather shocked. He'd never met another puffin like Greg, but Sally spoke up.

"Greg," she said, "I'm sure Peter was just being friendly!"

"Well," Greg replied, "I don't think so! It's not very nice sneezing over another puffin."

"At least he tried to bring me a present," Sally said. "I haven't noticed any presents from you!"

Greg didn't know what to say. He hadn't even thought about bringing Sally a present. He realised that Sally seemed to quite like Peter.

Peter was becoming a rival for Sally's attention. What could Greg do to save the day?

Meanwhile Sally enjoyed being the centre of attention. She was determined to make the most of it.

"I think Peter should be given the chance to prove himself," Sally suggested.

Greg decided that he needed to do something quickly. He looked at Peter carefully and then he had an idea.

"In that case I challenge you, Peter, to a contest," he suggested, "a fair fight with Sally as the prize for the winner. What do you say?"

"What a good idea!" Sally replied. The idea that two puffins were going to fight over her, made her feel very important.

Peter was not so sure. Greg was a very large puffin and probably much stronger than Peter. He remembered watching the two puffins fighting last year. It had appeared to be very nasty.

Peter looked at Sally. She was a very beautiful puffin, but was she worth fighting for? Peter thought she was very nice, but he wasn't attracted to her in the same way as he'd been to his lovely Ellie.

Greg noticed that Peter was hesitating.

"Scared of losing are you?" He said with a chuckle.

Peter began to feel very embarrassed. He really

didn't want to fight but a large group of puffins had gathered to see what was going on. He was being made to feel very cowardly in front of all the other puffins.

"OK, then," he said eventually. "If that's what Sally wants, I'm ready to fight."

Peter wasn't actually ready to fight at all, but he couldn't see any way out.

Peter and Greg were getting themselves ready when a familiar voice piped up. "Wait!"

Peter looked round to see that Holly had joined the group. He was very relieved to see her and hoped that she could come up with one of her clever ideas. She didn't let him down!

"Sally doesn't want a puffin who's good at fighting," Holly explained. "She needs one that can catch lots of food, so that he'll be able to take care of her and her pufflings. I suggest that instead of a fight, there should be a fishing competition. Whichever puffin can bring back the most sand eels will win."

"That sounds like a good idea!" Sally replied. "It does make a lot more sense."

Although the idea of a fight had been quite exciting, Sally didn't really want the two puffins to hurt each other, so she thought the idea of a fishing competition was great. Sally could still enjoy being the centre of attention.

Greg was furious and scowled menacingly, but he realised that it was no good arguing or he might lose Sally altogether. Peter was very relieved because he'd become quite good at fishing. Anything was better than a fight!

"Thanks Holly," he whispered quietly in her ear. She really did come up with some very good ideas. He wondered why he couldn't do the same. There always seemed to be snags with his plans.

It was all arranged. Peter and Greg would fly out to sea and catch as many sand eels as possible. The two puffins lined up side by side. Peter suddenly noticed that Greg had a strange sort of smile on his face. He had obviously thought of something. What was he planning?

"Are you ready?" Sally asked the two puffins.

"Yes!" they replied.

"Go!" she yelled.

Both puffins flew off together. Peter had hoped that they would separate because he was already very suspicious about Greg. Wherever Peter went, however, Greg wasn't far behind, so Peter decided to ignore him.

Peter soon found a large group of sand eels and so

he started fishing. He was very surprised to see Greg sitting on the surface of the water doing absolutely nothing. By now Peter was very worried. He was certain that Greg wasn't going to let him win, but why wasn't he fishing?

Peter decided to concentrate on the fishing. When Peter's bill was stuffed full with as many sand eels as possible, he decided to leave the water and fly back to Sally. Just as he managed to fly off the water, Peter noticed Greg leaving the water at the same time.

What happened next took Peter completely by surprise. Greg flew straight at Peter and knocked him back on to the water. The force of the ambush was so great that Peter dropped all the sand eels he'd caught. While Peter was trying to recover from the shock of the attack, Greg gratefully scooped up all Peter's sand eels and disappeared. The incident had happened so quickly that Peter had had no time to do anything about it.

Peter realised that he'd have to start again. There was a lot to do if he was going to catch more sand eels than he'd had before the ambush. He swam as fast as he could, trying to catch as many as possible. He was exhausted but he managed to catch quite a few.

As he was about to take off from the water for the final time, he made out a dark shape moving purposefully beneath him. It was a seal. Peter remembered that Grandad had said that seals could be dangerous at this time of year. The seal didn't seem to have noticed Peter but something had certainly caught its attention.

There were a few puffins around. Most had left the water. Then Peter suddenly noticed one puffin swimming around on the surface obviously enjoying itself. It was totally unaware of the danger underneath the water.

Peter knew exactly what he had to do. He dropped all the sand eels and flew as fast as he could towards the puffin. He realised that this would mean losing the fishing contest, but he also remembered what had happened to Ellie. He was determined not to see another puffin lost to any creature. As he approached the puffin he yelled at it.

"Fly! Now!" he screamed.

The poor puffin was so startled that it responded immediately to Peter's cry and not a moment too soon. As the puffin left the water, the seal's snout broke the surface. The puffin was just out of reach and managed to escape in the nick of time.

Peter flew with the puffin to the safety of the cliff top. Peter was relieved that he'd saved the puffin from certain death but he was also rather annoyed that this had caused him to lose the fishing contest. He decided that he ought to warn the puffin about the seals, but it was the other puffin who spoke first when they landed.

"I don't know how to thank you," the puffin spluttered. "I just wasn't thinking. You are so very brave and kind."

Peter opened his mouth to reply and realised there was something vaguely familiar about this puffin. He didn't know why but he thought he'd met it before. He also noticed that, despite being foolish, the puffin was a very cute female. Peter couldn't bring himself to show his anger.

As the puffin left the water, the seal's snout broke the surface.

Suddenly Peter began to feel the same way as he had when he had first met Ellie. What was it about this puffin? He decided to say nothing more. He had to get back to Sally and the other puffins.

"That's OK," he mumbled. "Just be more careful next time."

He flew back to where Sally and the others were waiting for him. Greg had been back for some time. When Peter appeared with no sand eels, they all wondered what he'd been doing. Even Greg had expected Peter to have caught a few.

"Not much good at fishing, then are you?" Greg chuckled. "Couldn't you find any?"

"Yes, where are your sand eels?" Sally asked him. "Greg managed to find quite a few."

Peter looked at Greg. "I know exactly where he found them," Peter thought.

"I just had a bad day," Peter replied not wanting to explain all that had happened.

Apart from being made to look rather silly in front of the other puffins, Peter was actually not that worried about losing the contest. Sally was certainly a beautiful puffin, but Peter was now far more interested in the puffin he'd just rescued. If Sally wanted Greg, she could have him.

"It looks like the best puffin has won the contest," Greg said jubilantly. "I'm sure that Sally and I will be very happy together."

Sally was quite content. Greg had won and that was that. She had no idea why Peter had failed so miserably, but that didn't really bother her.

Once the group had broken up, Holly who'd been joined by Ricky came over to Peter to ask him what had really happened.

"Peter, what happened?" Holly asked. "I was certain that you'd win a fishing competition very easily. That's why I suggested the idea in the first place."

Peter told them about the contest, how Greg had stolen his fish and then about the rescue of the puffin.

"I think we should tell Sally exactly what happened." Holly said. "The whole contest was unfair, Greg cheated and you saved the life of a puffin."

"No, please don't," Peter replied. "It'll cause too much trouble. Anyway there's no particular reason why she should believe me. It's Greg's word against mine."

Both Holly and Ricky stared at Peter in amazement. They couldn't understand why he wasn't that bothered about losing Sally to Greg.

"Peter," Holly asked. "Is there something you aren't telling us?"

Peter smiled. "Actually, there is!" He then went on to explain the strange feeling he'd had when the puffin that he'd rescued had first spoken to him.

Holly and Ricky also smiled.

"I see!" Holly replied. "I think I'm going to find out a little more about this puffin. I'm sure she'd be very happy to meet you again, Peter."

Peter blushed. He knew that he would very much like to meet the puffin again!

If anyone could find the puffin, Holly could! She had this knack of solving problems!

The next day when Peter flew back to the clifftop having spent the night at sea, he found a very excited Holly and Ricky waiting for him.

"Peter," she said, "I've discovered something really amazing."

"What's that?" Peter asked, keen to hear what Holly had to say.

"About the puffin you rescued yesterday," she started to explain.

"What about the puffin?" Peter inquired.

"Her name is Becky and she's Ellie's younger

sister!" Holly announced.

"What!" Peter exclaimed. "That's extraordinary!"

"It's true!" Holly continued.

"That's so amazing!" Peter replied. "As soon as she spoke to me, I just knew there was something familiar about her."

"Anyway," Holly continued, "the news about your rescue has spread very quickly. Becky and her friends want to see you again."

"I can't wait to see them," Peter replied. Even thinking of Becky produced this wonderful feeling inside him.

"What are we waiting for?" Holly asked. "Let's go!"

"Just a moment!" Peter said. "Holly you're a wonderful, wonderful puffin. Thank you for everything you've done for me."

She blushed and smiled. Although Holly was definitely Ricky's special female puffin, she'd always had a soft spot for Peter and was determined to do everything she could to make him happy.

"Becky and her friends have just flown out to sea to find some food." Holly said. "Come on let's go and find them!"

Peter couldn't wait!

He felt those goose bumps (or was it puffin bumps?) again inside. The fact that he'd saved Ellie's sister was amazing. He was tingling all over and couldn't wait to meet up with Becky again. He was determined that nothing was going to stop her becoming his special female puffin. Holly, Ricky and Peter flew out to sea. It wasn't long before Holly spotted the group.

"There they are!" she said to Peter.
Peter had become very nervous during the short flight and made a complete mess of his landing, splashing Becky and the rest of the group. Becky and her friends giggled. They realised that Peter could be just as normal as the rest of them despite his wonderful rescue yesterday.

When he'd recovered from his terrible landing, Peter shook himself and spoke to Becky.

"I'm sorry about that," he remarked. "That wasn't part of the plan!"

"Don't worry," Becky replied. "Holly's told me all about you and I think you're wonderful."

Peter blushed. He felt very embarrassed in front of the other puffins. He looked at Becky. That wonderful feeling of warmth and happiness came

Lightning Source UK Ltd.
Milton Keynes UK
UKOW03f1346180814

237111UK00002B/6/P